My Journey to Destiny

&

Spiritual Awakening

Gregg Smith

PAGE PUBLISHING
Conneaut Lake, PA

First originally published by
Page Publishing 2024

ISBN 979-8-88960-629-1 (pbk)
ISBN 979-8-88960-634-5 (digital)

Printed in the United States of America

Contents

Introduction..v
Chapter 1: The Beginning of a Miracle....1
Chapter 2: Temptations
            (Consciousness vs. Ego)........6
Chapter 3: College and Heaven 14
Chapter 4: Investment 18
Chapter 5: The Rebirth 22
Chapter 6: Discipline............................26
Chapter 7: The Soul 30
Chapter 8: Visions 34
Chapter 9: Manifestation 43
Chapter 10: A Space in Time 50

Introduction

Since birth, the ordinary repose of the subconscious submerges the will and purpose for
its desired destination. We as humans have
the power of choice and free will to take on
the many characteristics that challenge the
soul's purpose. We take on numerous paths
that direct a glimpse of said purpose destination. These journeys depict what's favorable,
warnings, upheavals, and prosperity. Since
the soul is the said guide for our feelings
and sense radar, we constructively ignore the
detailed act of being our true natural selves
to become a reality of reality acting in accord

with what's seen and how it can be seen. We, therefore, now have allowed our soul to train a thought of mental capacity different from its initial intent to feel. This thought process has given birth to a whole new reality of falsehood differing from which it came; therefore, leaving an unmasked reality dormant of its true inheritance, intentions, and bestowed guidance. *My Journey to Destiny & Spiritual Awakening* allowed me to lift the veil of falsehood while transforming the migration of mirrored cycle thoughts. My journey will describe the mere occurrences in one's life to transcend back to their true inhabitants through the many experiences we derive for listening purpose to awakening what's dormant. Leave the mask, masked, and reveal the unmasked undertaking for its true destiny which was promised to us all at birth.

God reveals himself to us through us. Allow iron to sharpen iron. Be an absorber of his grace, not an observer of his grace.

The Beginning of a Miracle

I must say my journey started in my subconscious well before July 15, 2003. On that day, I was convicted of armed bank robbery, conspiracy, and brandishing a firearm during crime and violence. That day, I was sentenced to 130 months at the federal bureau of prisons. Whereas it's told many times by people this common theme, tell me the truth, I want to know the truth. Show me the truth in every aspect of my life. Often than none, there's always the perception to hear a lie. Why? Because it sounds better, and it's more believable because of the contrast between the speaker submitting what's readily accepted by the world and what's commonly known and taught. My journey to destiny & spiritual awakening will provide the reader with unbelievable truths that manifested themselves during my day-to-day travels during this transformation. Many would say and believe the saying, "If I told you the truth, you wouldn't believe me anyway." I'm going to tell and explain the miracle behind spiritual awakening and its powerful force. Upon arrival at FCI ELKTON, I was encountered by two men that would change my life and path as it is today (Michael Crowell and Henry Montalvo). Destiny was preset before, during, and after my trial hearing. What I didn't know or understand at the time was synchronicities were occurring without my knowledge or comprehension—a trinity within the presence of my life. My subconscious knew beforehand what it wanted and what it wanted me to be. The Beginning of my trinity (knowledge of self, father of self, and man of self). Alexander Williams Jr., the processor of the second act of this trinity, being during the aspect of this metamorphosis putting action behind, said path provided wisdom to come about, being the son of the divine while recognizing the woman, finimine energy is the protector. Mike and Henry, on the third and final part of this trinity, provided guidance being the effect that completes the teaching, so I can be readily yoked for the transformation (have understanding, inheriting the holy spirit while being the child of God). Before I could understand anything that was taking place in my life, I must first understand the synchronicities and the remembrance of like events and occurrences that were happening in my life. Like why? what? and how?

I was born on May 8, 1971. It was no coincidence the judge presiding over my case, the Honorable Alexander Williams Jr., was born on May 8, 1948. Henry Montalvo's *How to Be Gone in His Spiritual Aspect* was released from prison on May 8, 2006, three years after I got there and met him. Things began to change and took shape beyond my realm and ethereal understanding. All I know was I was witnessing the symbolic transmission of the three channels life has to offer. Universal family in all phases in the world we live in today—mind, body, and soul; solid, liquid, and gas; freedom, justice, and equality; food, clothing, and shelter; width, depth, and heights. Throughout this process, metaphysics was taken into account—ontology, cosmology, epistemology, philosophy, and aesthetics. Therefore, a concept was given that we are here to be a distributor of God's power; we must be that through which God may express. We are here to rediscover ourselves. We have been living in an imaginary world. Our purpose is to awaken the real world. Do this and the mission of the master within can begin. People will then see us in a new light. They will sense a great change in us because we are becoming *us*. We cannot take credit for it. It's the father within who is doing the work and if our personal ego expands it will fill the channel and shut off the flow. All the entities throughout the universe, including *us*, were created for just one purpose. To have constant intercommunion with the God self to be a channel for his manifestation. My "journey to destiny and spiritual awakening" starts here.

CHAPTER 2

Temptations
(Consciousness vs. Ego)

I'm having a harder time than usual remaining peaceful. In the interest of helping me cope with my emotional contradictions, I'm asking you to provide me with the clarity and open-mindedness to write an in-depth piece about my inward struggle. This piece would chronicle the psychological competition that I engage myself in behind the storylines. Sometimes I have problems accepting authority; other times the problem is not being an authority. The only solution is to put me under the sharpest knife, which is the pen. As you well know, these past few years have been fully loaded with learning experiences that were very difficult for me to overcome. In the world, I did a lot of harmful things because I was good at them not because I liked them. I was consistent, and I thought I could never fail. But today, I'm dealing with dark issues. I don't feel like advocating peace. I wanna push somebody out of the picture. Finished a war that the other man started. The story is an outline describing old habits that are easy to explain but hard to break. The objective is not to glorify past wars I've miserably lost but to examine new challenges that threaten to prevent me from writing my true success story. Remember the day I said I will rather be famous than rich and if given the choice between love and respect? I'd rather be loved. My story revealed the brash and cocky persona I've adopted to obtain both of those jewels, and at the same time, neglecting my inner self. I've lived a life as a wounded healer, from a kind-hearted kid to a crazy mind criminal. *Please* know that I'm not complaining. I just want to admit to you and myself that I've selflessly misused your gifts for cheap thrills. There's an ongoing struggle inside me where temptation fights against my spiritual principles. And through the constant introspection I've acquired. I've been able to find my true essence, and I am no longer a stranger to my inner self. Just like everyone else, my soul possesses both the beauty and the brutality of nature. The good boss wants to be the most of everything. The most lovable, courageous, accepted, just, and respected. The bad boss wants to get the most out of everything and everyone through fear. Most of the action in the epic saga I'm about to write takes place doing a by-myself meeting of the minds; upon a road less travel, gather some of your greatest messengers—Abraham, Moses, Job, Solomon, Peter, Paul, and John. These are my spiritual counselors who provide me with GOD (good ordinary direction). The GOD squad stands ready to defend the faith on the right side of the road. To my left stand Capone, Bugsy, Nitty, Meyer Sinatra, and Lucky Giancana. They're known as the MOB (murder our brothers), and they take the position of offense. These two sides of myself standing on the line separated only by conscience. The die is cast. Someone has murdered a big member of my team. There is no need for justice for the MOB react and classic faction.

"Break the guy's face!" says boot. Without a thought. I nod in agreement, but then Solomon intervenes with his wisdom, saying only "A fool pays back bad for bad."

He moves for a dismissal acquittal. Paul seconds the motion and invites me to stand next to him on the decision. But before I can turn and step over the line, Capone pulls out the heat, grabs me by the arm, and shouts, "Get lost! He's ours." Then he whispers in my ear. "They made you, but we train you." That's when I cross the line. Not because it's a good idea but for reasons of ego. To show that I'm used to displaying negative power without thinking twice, for a crook with a conscious, the road less traveled can be an extremely perilous street. I once wrote *American Inc. Love a Tough Guy*, but America isn't represented on my counsel. You are. Through characters and principles that I loved and respected but don't always uphold. The power and responsibility of decision is my hand every minute of the day. One hand represents caring, attention, affection, appreciation, and love, on the other. There's lust, greed, passion, desire, and sin. The question is, which hand will grip the pen? This is exactly why I'm proposing this story. You've bought me through the difficulties, helped me to appreciate discipline, learned from it, and encouraged others to do the same. Now I want to tell my story. Let my closest friends and even closer enemies know that I'm not as tough as I seem or, perhaps, would like to be. Let them know that if I ever close my eyes and ears to reason, the chances of having an out-of-mind experience and somewhere between hell and yeah! Just give me the go-ahead, and I'll write the truth! What problems arise when I'm always thinking tough? The roughneck routine used to be a defense mechanism, and then it became an addiction to pain. Each day, I am forced to go to war with my most incomparable foe—the person I was yesterday. The unusual suspect does minor things to irritate me, like giving an overconfident facial in the morning's reflection. It's him I must grapple with when I turn off the Mac, close my mouth, put away the motivational memoirs, and stare down destiny. I want to expose that person on paper but not with the intention of validating my irrationality or gaining sympathetic impressions from those who never liked or understood me. Why then? So that the rest of my perilous street team can't identify the real enemy. My true adversary doesn't have pale skin to me because of a lack of melanin. He doesn't pass me over for promotions. He can hear everything I say yet cannot read my mind. He can influence me only if I'm harboring a desire to backslide. If he were to read this writing, he would be totally clueless as to what it is I'm talking about, although you understand it. The person I've become, I'm happy to say, is constantly helping people to help themselves. My question is this; How can I use the passionate energy you bless me with to involve others in this story, and how can I prevent injustices toward myself and those I love to reinvent my old personality? The one that cares more about respect than love? There is a lot of being human being. I'd rather be a human. Help me do the right thing.

CHAPTER 3
College and Heaven

Why is education furthered? What is it? Why is it worth it? How does it benefit me?

Knowledge is a form of education. Wisdom is knowledge formed. Understanding is the expansion of the mind experiencing and opening of major energy points within the chakras so the imagination can increase the knowledge it obtained throughout its existence. In short, it details the arrival of one shortcoming, enlightening the thought process to understand that where logic stops, the imagination begins, and so does creation and the ability to receive and be a part of creation. Everyone is not going to get it, but everyone feels they have it. It's not for all to get because some of us are examples and vessels that emit his light transparent in different areas. Only in the realm of true enlightenment and spiritual guidance will his presence be felt and acted upon and divinely understood. When it comes to college and heaven, one must also decide on a course of action. Do I want to continue my education by going to college on this physical plane, or do I want to evolve, becoming the best version of myself while here on earth? First, having a good instinctive reason to question and seek answers is a start. When that occurs, the senses can never be satisfied even after the continuous supply of sensory. The ocean can only be filled with a continuous supply of water. You are only limited by the questions unasked or answers not acted upon. Few people alive drink in everything around them. They consume experiences and things and turn that fuel into something else. The number changes, but the formula remains the same. So whatever that something, maybe it should have your fingerprints on it. If you don't do that, you will be living, but you won't be alive. Information is the key to personal and political freedom and wealth. The value of information weighs nothing and everything at the same time. One must trade it with caution and care. Lock!

Remain focused on the key, not the locks. Locks are another form of numbers that constantly change. The master key to the one who holds it will unlock them all. Words and information are the keys. Ideas are important. Principles are important. Words are important, but your word is the most important of all. Your word is who you are and what represents you. Not everyone is going to college, and not everyone is going to heaven. Which do you prefer?

CHAPTER 4

Investment

We as humans look at and see life from different cultures, experiences, and perspectives—religion, mystery, myths, and innate belief systems. It's an investment of life in which one perceives what they want out of every situation or occurrence, providing the ego or heart. Being observant or not making investments knowledgeable from within or what they experience and want it to be, making life and its occurrences and situations adorable or unpleasant.

Investing in any aspect of life takes obedience, willingness, and the necessary determination to succeed. Such investments include love, time money, and property. Investing is not probable without self-insight. The ultimate investment is self-worth, self-seeking, and self-sacrifice. We cannot invest tangibly without self-knowing. Many people invest in love without self-evaluation, not readily putting into the depths of their internal desires. They substitute such desires for the thought of love and not its true intentions. It's a false sense of feeling, not a desire but a carnal understanding of want. Through the years, the time has passed and minds have grown, leaving marked impressions on one's head and heart. In evaluating and acknowledging love, the value has been tested in a realm of catastrophic beginnings and endings and favorable conditions beginning and endings. Therefore, unprecedented decisions to continue this valuable asset leads to investing boundaries between disparities and misfortune due to life and its perplexities.

Time is the primal aspect of investing in one's existing state of being. Since we all share the same twenty-four hours of the day, it's evident that investing our time in the highest level of self-being will reflect in the space occupied by us. Everything we perceive comes in time or within time. Time is a necessity with what's inevitable. Remember the saying, "Everything happens in due time." Time provides healing, nourishment, growth, and potential. Time is an unavoidable investment that we must all declare.

Money and property are tangible results of investing. The process of coping with this internal structure defies and defines the empowerment of one's true essence and growth. Being able to recognize this frequent occurrence brings the individual closer to self-realization and self-investing. This blind leap of faith, therefore, unrealized beforehand and unused, is a force tapped into the self-consciousness by investing into the investment of self. As we go deep inside ourselves, there we find such a beautiful space within. We actually see the divine investment which supports our lives. Investing in this experience drops the veil of our egos so we can invest in our own perfection. So the true secret to investing in life is that we are not only enough; we are actually all there is.

CHAPTER 5

The Rebirth

Rebirth inception ignites with a shock that revolutionizes life interests within a direction contrary to one's ambition. There are all types of catastrophes that provoke the change to reawaken the rebirth of existence. Leaving one conscious state to another transforming migrational states of wanting to become proactive in aspects of healing, the mind's intentions separate from negative thoughts and feelings into a more positive sense to be impactful toward reciprocity and all that exists. Not everyone wants or considers themselves spiritual, but they are. We are born with its identity and, therefore, carry vigor bestowed in the heart in every thought and action we take upon our life and journey. In comparison, everyone considers themselves special in some way. The only difference is no difference at all.

There's an immanent confidant in us all—the one we listen to when we want to feel good and the one we listen to when we want to ignore in times of sorrow or disbelief. Therefore, the power of choice and will bounds what we wanna be or not believe. In this stage of rebirth, we are in constant reincarnation with every changing thought process and pattern. The moment we change a thought, change a perception, or change in any form, it is a rebirth of our existing condition. It's a known fact that we can't experience what we experienced a second ago. We can rediscover the moment but not share it in the same form in its entirety. A new us has submerged from the second after its birth state to engage upon another birth reality—he ever existence of rebirth and reincarnation. As we reinvent ourselves while emerging into the authentic self, people's situations and currencies become loved because we're experiencing the oneness in our environment. Vitality is stretched beyond dynamic structure, therefore realizing its force. Can you imagine loving all the time despite trouble and difficulties being thrown at you constantly? Vitality in this stage of rebirth has no fears, no worries, and no shame. You're not ashamed to be criticized, ridiculed, or condemned in any form. You have transformed from the polarity of what's negative and positive, therefore transmitting an energy of oneness, demonstrating and accepting beauty in all things, people, situations, and occurrences. Since love can be shown in the physical presence to show happiness, sorrow, and grief, this stage of rebirth has no outer manifestation of such. Its powerful influence displays no emotional contradictions expenditures, although caring and feeling empathy bestows it accepting the mental aspects of those who are immediately in their vicinity, taking on energies of suffering depression within their embodiment to release a vibration of frequency different from their own, consequently relinquishes an infinite source of an abundance of love and its vital to restoring the passage much as regenerating rebirth within the atmosphere from which it came. So for the man who has found the truth, new suffering awaits him when he finds the path to eternity and the undertaking of infinite thought through his/her rebirth.

CHAPTER 6

Discipline

Discipline enforces obedience and instruction all while training through a form of punishment. Discipline is the fear that takes us through life barriers we wouldn't take ourselves through. It is just areas in life that protrude diligence, determination, and reliability all while being industrious and also being averse to correcting pessimism, inflexibility, and selfishness. The force decorates interception of what's perceived by the want and occurrence providing the satisfaction of the ego. The ego is a baby/child thought that plays the mind against the heart just as an infant/child would do to get its way. Every human has experienced a child crying or enacting a behavior to get what he or she wanted to satisfy his ego. Or was it the ego or internal satisfaction that illuminated the change, want, or desire? Since a child/infant can't discern its compass, therefore, the diligence and determination of the parents' observance exuberate the knowledge from discipline over a period of time to make a firm and industrious decision that solidifies the reliability within the self-discipline. Situations will arise with unpleasant and adorable externalizations, not intrinsic or essential without even realizing its initiations stage a situation within his/her becomes a questionable waving of misunderstandings of his/her belief. An ascension of confusion infiltrates the listening to within to assimilate a false understanding to conquer and conform the inner will and digest what is real and felt, and what is negative and false. Facts and accumulations from within will devour the prowess from patience and tolerance to withstand conflicts of interest and confidence to succeed. All this can be infringed upon by lack of knowledge and lack of what's perceived. Discipline only acknowledged participation and patience. It knows no other boundaries or barriers. It can't be manipulated because of its creative barriers. How many times have you thought you had it your way, let's say, in the bag? But somehow, it came back to bite what you call out the ass. Discipline is mirrored images of what one perceives without its total influence and instruction. How can one yet not be a saint and want another to be? How can he/she prove, and how can he/she teach? It's not easy to discipline ourselves without obedience. So what is discipline, and how can one obtain it? It's the thought of suffering, failure, and thoughts of not believing in the understanding of what self can achieve without the acceptance of others, so I, you, the individual can prosper in the light and understanding from within.

CHAPTER 7

The Soul

The true prophecy is to see, grow, and prosper every thought of uncertainty crossing one path of subconscious reason or obscurity being the motive before the motive, the act before the enactment, and the message before the sender. In many ways, soul clarity has its ways of making an expression felt and experienced through the light of what's reflected by the synergies in one's character apart from any environment, which depicts the person's past or present encounters. Life's darkest and most illuminated secrets are revealed in the soul. This realm brings the unconscious and conscious. It inspires principles like, I am action, resistance, completion, and results, all while demonstrating the law of polarity (positive, negative, initiative, receptive, masculine, and feminine). The soul is definitely predicated on the self and attributes of one's own desires. Life-driven dreams are the cognition of competitive natures that serve what's considered inner peace until it's actually found. Why? The soul is infinite, but it can't actually serve a purpose until it is identified by its user/owner. Imagine owning and building your own custom-made car but never driving it. You possess it, want it, and have it but don't understand all its features or have even driven it because you didn't put it to use yet. Custom design made for you, but you haven't experienced any or all the features and never will. Like the car upon experiencing it, you may use certain features and may not use some at all. Whereas the soul has unlimited features—infinite features that are infectious to the mind and body and ready to use when needed but are never applied because they're not readily identified by its owner. Here we have an ego carnal understanding against a spiritual want and desire. The soul only rests on the desires of what's good and universal essence, while the ego rests on its desire to please the senses, not knowing the soul. The sole purpose is to grant the individual and entity infinite abundance and all that exists. Therefore, we lack the essential principles in the ego to conform to what's unseen because of the lack of depth used by the soul. The soul has thousands of years of information to give versus the smidgen of years the human body provides. Its source amplifies knowledge from past generations and eons of resourcefulness.

It's the center of knowledge for men and women. The soul is the direct perception of the truth in life as it exists today and forever.

CHAPTER 8

Visions

We draw people to try and see our visions and want clarity from them *to* justify our authority or personification. God's vision resides in simplicity, not complexity. It's important to remember the essence of life that the same divine consciousness exists equally as everything. When we look into any pair of eyes, we see the same consciousness gazing back at us. It is like looking into a mirror and seeing our own reflection. There is only one perceiver. We must remember we are always the seer and never the seen. The seen has to do with the ego. The seer is the self. When we look out and perceive what is, we are experiencing being the seer.

If, however, we are conscious of ourselves being the one who is seen, the one looked at, the one perceived, then we are experiencing the ego. The ego thinks there is another seer in someone else who is capable of seeing us, thinking things about us, feeling things about us, having opinions of us, and so forth. The scene is a force that conceals the ultimate truth. This includes anything that can be seen about us. What is real about us can't be seen with our physical eyes. It can only be experienced. No one else can see the reality of us. They can only experience that reality within themselves. This is very important to understand. The only way to know the truth of another is to know the truth of our own self. Since we share the same self, to see the reality is not to see another at all, but it is to experience that truth within ourselves. Remember, life is a series of incarnations, each taken up where the other left off. When we realized this life is only another day in the life of the soul, a certain detachment arises regarding everyday details. Each day, I read the scriptures. I'm reminded that many people have very hard lives and have to go through things that no one would look forward to. The fact is, we can have a hard incarnation just like we have a bad day. Over the eons of incarnations so much, karma has been accumulated, and it must be dissolved by grace and through the fire of meditation before liberation. You see, hard times push us through barriers that we would never push through if life was easy or comfortable. On the other hand, on the scale of spiritual evolution, it isn't that each life is easier or more desirable than the one before. As we evolve spiritually, more is expected of us. We may have to face tests and obstacles that we only now have the capacity to deal with. Imagine every few saints and masters had easy lives. To look at the lives of great beings, we see that they face one challenge after another. Often, they were persecuted, condemned, or crucified. It's not that they were publicly congratulated and honored for their attainment. So it's not that we can look at our life and think, *Is this all I've managed to accomplish after eons of incarnations? Is this as far as I've managed to get? Everything has led up to this?* We may have already experienced the things we fantasize about. We may have had wealth, prestige, stature, and admirers. We're probably already done and had all the things we desperately wish we could do, and one reason we might desire something now is the subtle memory of it in a past life, which we have gotten used to remembering. We might not understand that our soul chose an incarnation of the tapestry for spiritual growth.

Sooner or later, we have to stop and ask ourselves really why we are here. Do we want an ideal life according to our own conditioned standards, a perfect arrangement of truth? Or do we want to be liberated? Liberation implies liberation from this karma. Pursuing a different life with new and improved karma only leads to another incarnation. You see, all our desires can be fulfilled, only not in this lifetime. It's not part of the karmic plan, and besides, one incarnation doesn't last long enough. If we can't get free from our desires and we end this incarnation clinging to them, then we will come back to another body so that those desires can be fulfilled. Is it worth it? Obviously, most people think so, for they keep coming back for life after life, never getting enough of this world, never getting enough money, sex, power, gratification, and respect for whatever they think this world has to offer. Tell me, do you want to fulfill your desires or to be liberated? We can't have both. We have to decide clearly which we want, which is our greatest priority, and then live with that choice without wavering back and forth. Liberation includes the complete acceptance of all that exists right now. We are bound to whatever we can't accept. Once we accept it, we can be free from it. The best thing to do with a problem, for example, is simply to allow space for it, to let it be. This doesn't mean to condone or justify it. It simply means to come into harmony with it. From this point, it can more easily be changed or eliminated. By denying it, rejecting it, fighting it, or complaining about it, we often only perpetuate it. For example, say we are married and there is something we don't like about our partner. If we make a big issue of it and try to change our partner and then get upset when our partner doesn't change to suit our own standards, then we have a problem. Such problems destroyed many otherwise good relationships, and no doubt, we will blame this on our partner. He/she never did what I wanted him/her to. He/she never became what I wanted her/him to become, he/she never changed in the ways I insisted that he/she changed, so I divorced him/her. She/he deserved it. If he/she really loved me, he/she would have become what I wanted him/her to be. On the other hand, we can simply come into harmony with what is difficult to accept. We can understand that this is how he or she is, that he or she has his or her own karma to go through, his or her own thoughts to work out, and that it is not our responsibility to force him or her to change or improve. Who are we to be irritated or annoyed at someone else we claim to love? What ego is it to disapprove of? Are we going to get mad at another's karma? Are we going to be angry with his or her past experiences or thoughts? Even if he or she wanted to change, what could he or she do? Much discipline is required to get free from thoughts. We can't just drop them because someone else disapproves, as much as we might like to. If a couple is on the same accord, they each have some idea of what the other needs to work on. The way to help each other is to allow the other the space to work it out and to be supportive without condoning what needs to be changed. We can say we can get through this together. We can help each other. The worst thing is to criticize and condemn each other. Can't you give up your desires? Can't you drop your anger?

No, if these things could be so easily given up, we wouldn't have to discipline ourselves. In relationships, we must allow space for that time to practice discipline. We can't criticize a person for not yet being a saint. In the same way, we shouldn't criticize ourselves in our own life. We shouldn't always be thinking of how things aren't so good or how things could be better. If things were better, it wouldn't help anything. What we need is to experience the truth. Only when we experience the truth do we see everything as it is. Only then can we relax and enjoy ourselves. Only then can we constantly delight in the world and in other people. Only then will we experience perpetual love. Only then will we experience freedom. Only then is their contentment, fulfillment, and purpose in this life.

CHAPTER 9

Manifestation

Manifestation can be seen in all that exists visibly or invisibly. Let's take a banana, for example, which is born green, ripe in the middle when yellow, dies rotten when brown. Some of today's manifestations are empowered and taught without divine research or integrity. Skimming the surface to ignite chaos and confusion. Solutions are made declaratory and not culpable to fit in and serve an objective purpose. Manifestation brings aspirations, generalizations, and expectations along with perceptions and realizations. We seek these manifestations through cultures, experiences, religions, mysteries, myths, and inner belief systems. The formula for this brings about different manifestations based on the thought conceived from the process one adheres to produce the required result pinpointing the barriers surrounding his or her actions to manifest. How do we do that? There are two aspects to consider (feeling and thought). A feeling way of doing something versus a thoughtful way of doing things. This is a process used by all that nets different results in its form. Manifestation derives from the act, process, perceived inwardly and outwardly to influence perceptible expressions toward visible and invisible entities. The feeling aspect provides the perceived course of action or belief taken. Internalize assimilations—the formula for its power. Feelings are the invisible inspired influence. The thought aspect process is perceptible based on theory, practice, and reason to influence visible thought expressions. Let's say we want to manifest forgiveness using the formulas for thought and feelings. The common says, just forgive and forget. Using the thought process basically brings about a reasonable outcome of acceptance perceived beyond the event or occurrence in a plan on intention to produce outward impressions. The thought replays the action over again before it can yield a result through practice and reason; therefore, the reaction is to manifest forgiveness expressed in apologies. Using feelings to forgive, its influence is invisible knowing only to be. Persistence in every manner, its power is unseen, unheard, and unrealized by the receiver who expects a verbal apology. This force empowers what is remembered, learned healed, and released without action. Its inward phenomenon directs the sensory experience in the heart that is not infiltrated by thought without outward actions taken. So what needs to be forgiven is already forgiven and forgotten. The manifestations of apologies viable of feelings and thought, first, what is an apology? Is it something God gives freely or ordains or something the human individual insists on or wants? Spiritual understanding knows that all actions are destined to provide clarity of clairvoyant beyond reasonable perception. So to satisfy the thought intentions separate from the feelings, we ask for apologies or expect them to gratify the thought and not feelings intent to influence. Does it really comfort the just cause or the innate ability at that instance? So if the feeling is constant and all-knowing, why would they apologize or expect an apology for just being and knowing for recognizing his own self? Creations forms in the thoughts and manifests in the physical. An apology is manifested to show forgiveness and such when it is actually a thought experienced. What happens when an apology is not accepted? Does it change the narrative? What actually happens when it's accepted? Does it change the experience? So how do personal perspectives outsource spiritual principles to uphold a nation and the body of human existence to be whole? Okay, say I render an apology to an individual as we all have throughout the acts of giving generosity and kindness. The fact is, at times, it was accepted, and at times, it wasn't, feeling it's all given at all times passively in abundance without vacillating its authority. Thoughts coming from the subconscious are conscious belief manifestations. Humans and animals are bestowed with instincts. The difference is animals rely on it more deeply because they can't perceive anything without concept as humans do, whereas the inheritance of choice, will, and ambition allows us to procreate, create, preserve, and foretell, if necessary, these determinations. How many of you planned a dinner date, party, or even called home to ask what's for lunch, breakfast, or dinner for manifestation? A necessity want and craving without fear or anxiety due to powers yielded to us. This power manifestation has a multitude of expressions one can experience. How about listening to understand? The faculty that exposes the same two words used. How can you listen without understanding, and how can you understand without listening? This shows the infiltration of what's established within and what it constitutes. A thought can reflect a feeling where a feeling describes an emotion but never adheres to the thought because the feeling is genuine and true in its ever existence. A feeling is always factual, whereas a thought isn't. Thought contains a duality of truth and falsity, whereas feeling contains all known facts considered of itself. On the other hand, thought can also manifest mistakes, joy, chaos, states of bliss, misfortune, etc., which all depend on the everlasting effect of its manifestation. Though it produces probabilities, feelings always produce divine results. Can a thought reveal inhabitants that can live without substance? Whereas feelings are their own.

Manifestations are nature's inhabitants without resources or the form from which it came.

CHAPTER 10

A Space in Time

How can we infiltrate our thoughts to go beyond the perception of another? Life is self at the moment, not recorded by the thought before or after the action. Individuals perceive the latter or look beforehand at what's to come or what could have or should have been. There is no clear representation or remedy to justify the density of not conducting a carnal reality. Life, as I experience it today, brings me to a crossroads of understanding. What once confused or irritated me becomes a humbling experience of what actually really separates from what was perceived or thought of. I realized I'm actually living life in the now, not past or future beliefs or wants. Living life in the now bestows a comfort of existence with existing realities beholding the natural flow of energy within its natural essence. The real question is, what can I give or establish from this reality? The only answer is a constant reality a constant realization. The ever now. What does it do? It raises or lowers the vibrations transmitted through the consciousness. As I've noticed, there are positive and negative responses due to postures driven by the thought. Consciously, we see this on a daily basis, whereas unconsciously this reality lies dormant, tucked away for its use.

Time has evolved in its own existence by way of experiencing itself. As it repeats itself, its existence is unknown—unknown in how it is used, unknown in its reaction, and unknown in its being. So to constantly adapt, it remains in the now. Being in the now, living in the now, believing in the now, accepting the now, whereas everything is, and that exists is the now. Have you ever treated a person better than they treated themselves in terms of respect, honor, and dignity, putting aside thought patterns of good for their highest good? I mean, being a catalyst for the things they don't understand and how to make use of a deity they think they don't possess. The mere fear of this apprehension conforms and conceals in the unjust and injustices we appropriate in our daily lives. Imagine feeling slighted by means of conversation respect, honor, and dignity in that precise order by a friend, loved one, or someone you appreciate, admire, and hold high regard for, and the feeling is not reciprocated, steaming from their spoken word to you in regard to their nature and not their essence and true intentions. You, on the other hand, know and understand their transformation hasn't occurred, so now you feel responsible for them and their actions. What's happening at that moment is your transmitting your light and energy of life and self-awareness living in a space in time. People always talk about action and what's shown. Action can deceive in ways, not how that person really feels. Actions can definitely depict a perception—a perception beyond belief and understanding to get a desired result. Typically, 90 percent of people I talk to define a person by their actions, which is a perceivable concept adopted by many. But what's not said is their understanding of why their disappointment arises from a soul not committed to self. The course of action taken to derive at the perception point. Whereas, on the other hand, when acceptance of these actions occurs, one perceives a state of understanding without question and without wondering from the root from which it came. Therefore, never realize the acceptance but embrace the reality without embracing its core substance. We readily experience this manifestation today in a space in time. Looking at myself from the inside out to become conscious, I had to see myself from both the outside and the inside out; therefore, recognizing the necessary changes, I desired to manifest a higher vibration to achieve my inner knowing and goals I couldn't attain in a lower vibration. It was a time in space when decisions were made for me by way of dishonesty. Living the truth and being in the now allows a person to decide their own fate. Has someone ever told you part of a situation or an occurrence? By doing that, the person has already made a decision for you based on how you will react, therefore taking away your free will to conduct a viable option for yourself, not readily giving you the opportunity to decide which direction you want to take. Here, I occupy a space in time with alternative realities—my past, my present, and my future. In these realities, the transformation has occurred in different stages for the many paths I can take. In my past, I couldn't represent the authentic me, whereas I didn't know him or how to find him. He was on a course of self-evolvement decorated by life treasures seen in others by others without recognition of spiritual cause and effect. The effect of being spiritual definitely subsides what's common. Why is it that common can't be reproduced in action but understood in sight? Sight becomes the master of what's seen, therefore overriding all its necessary essence to determine what's real, defying the ever-presence of what's felt. My present prescribes a resolution through my past failures, and believe me, the average life has plenty. Life past, present, and future has dualities that can't be unseen but definitely unrealized. It's definitely unrealized because the substance is clear. The substance will not let anyone understand because everyone can't go through the challenges they must face to apprehend their original character or being. If this was so, there wouldn't be things we disapprove of about our character. Representing my inner core supports my presence in a space in time. My future has beheld my past and present by what's given again or the path upon taken. I can choose to become my past self and continue past driven or present self to complete a journey. So destiny contributing result derived from a decision and course recognize past and present realities. What happens when your past doesn't respect your presence, and your presence doesn't respect your past? You cannot have a favorable future. My past prepared me for what I'm doing today, and my present represents me by way of description, and my future holds the light of promise forbearance in the actions, taking yielding fruit from its harvest. What difference can I expect from change? Everything compared to science gives us a competitive edge. Tangible things are results from what's within and scientifically sorted. What can be said about a space in time has already been done or said. Our continued action and process toward one's goals only reflect the past and the present. Since space is occupied by time and time defines space, what is it actually? We consume infinite space within infinite time. Time only measures the space we occupy. There's really no such understanding. It's only a feeling. Space and time emulate a place to and fro, whereas distance is reached. What if I told you that doesn't exist? Where is the time? Where is space? Space only occupies itself. Time is not occupied at all. Can you imagine having an out-of-body experience reflecting space and time? How would you describe its presence? What would it be like and where would you be? Only in the state of being and processing a mental image of what a space in time can be. The beginning of a miracle has taken place, temptation has risen, manifestations taking shape, visions occur while being, discipline in the matters of the soul arriving at investments points that took place in the midst of the rebirth while intuitively balancing college and heaven, looking through the lenses of a space in time.

About the Author

Gregg Smith is an author and motivational speaker who wants to inspire the world through his divine wisdom and personal insight. He graduated high school in 1990. A few years later, he was married with two kids. He had a career working for WMATA as a bus driver. On December 27, 2001, he opened three bank boxes brought to him by his friends. Those boxes would change his life. On July 15, 2003, he was sentenced to 130 months in the Federal Bureau of Prisons for conspiracy to armed bank robbery and brandishing a firearm during a crime and violence. He spent nine years and six months before he was released. He found spirituality while in prison from a man named Michael Crowell. As a direct result of him losing everything, including his wife and kids, he's been studying the metaphysical aspect of spirituality for twenty years now.